COUNTER-TERRORIST FORCES WITH THE CIA

Rescue and Prevention: Defending Our Nation

- Biological and Germ Warfare Protection
- Border and Immigration Control
- Counterterrorist Forces with the CIA
- The Department of Homeland Security
- The Drug Enforcement Administration
- Firefighters
- Hostage Rescue with the FBI
- The National Guard
- Police Crime Prevention
- Protecting the Nation with the U.S. Air Force
- Protecting the Nation with the U.S. Army
- Protecting the Nation with the U.S. Navy
- Rescue at Sea with the U.S. and Canadian Coast Guards
- The U.S. Transportation Security Administration
- Wilderness Rescue with the U.S. Search and Rescue Task Force

COUNTER-TERRORIST FORCES WITH THE CIA

JOHN WRIGHT

MASON CREST PUBLISHERS
www.masoncrest.com

Mason Crest Publishers Inc.
370 Reed Road
Broomall, PA 19008
(866) MCP-BOOK (toll free)
www.masoncrest.com

First printing

1 2 3 4 5 6 7 8 9 10

Library of Congress Cataloging-in-Publication Data on file
at the Library of Congress

ISBN 1-59084-407-6

Editorial and design by
Amber Books Ltd.
Bradley's Close
74–77 White Lion Street
London N1 9PF
www.amberbooks.co.uk

Project Editor: Michael Spilling
Design: Graham Curd
Picture Research: Natasha Jones

Printed and bound in Jordan

Picture credits
Corbis: 11; Popperfoto: 8, 15, 16, 20, 36, 50, 59, 63, 65, 71, 78, 83, 86; Topham Picturepoint: 6, 12, 14, 18, 19, 21, 22, 24, 26, 29, 30, 35, 40, 42, 44, 46, 52, 55, 64, 66, 73, 74, 77, 81, 82, 85, 89; The Picture Desk, Kobal Collection: 61; U.S. Department of Defense: 33, 45, 49, 54, 56, 68, 70; U.S. National Archives: 39.
Front cover: Popperfoto (center), Topham Picturepoint (top, bottom left, bottom right).

DEDICATION

This book is dedicated to those who perished in the terrorist attacks of September 11, 2001, and to all the committed individuals who continually serve to defend freedom and protect the American people.

CONTENTS

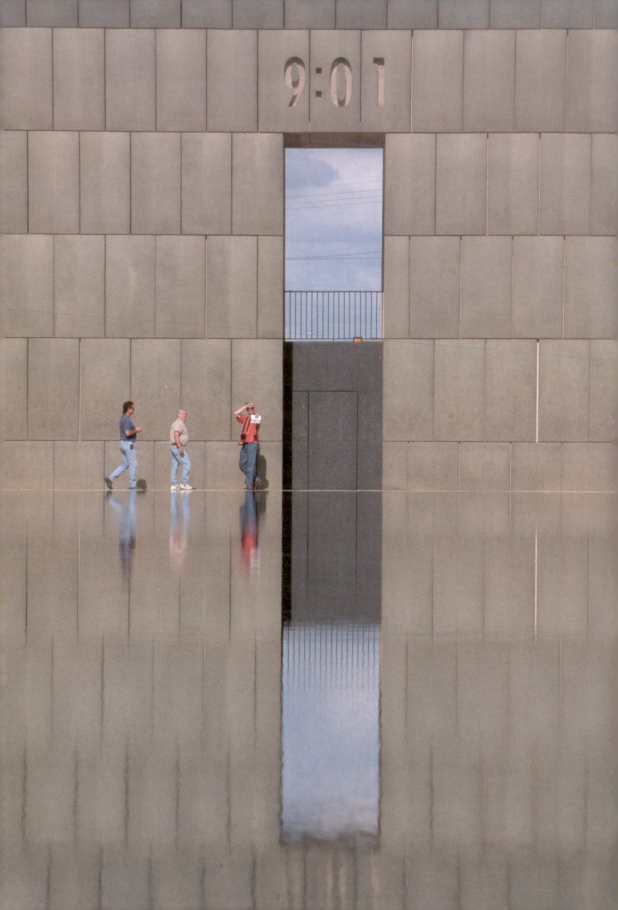

INTRODUCTION

September 11, 2001, saw terrorism cast its lethal shadow across the globe. The deaths inflicted at the Twin Towers, at the Pentagon, and in Pennsylvania were truly an attack on the world and civilization itself. However, even as the impact echoed around the world, the forces of decency were fighting back: Americans drew inspiration from a new breed of previously unsung, everyday heroes. Amid the smoking rubble, firefighters, police officers, search-and-rescue, and other "first responders" made history. The sacrifices made that day will never be forgotten.

Out of the horror and destruction, we have fought back on every front. When the terrorists struck, their target was not just the United States, but also the values that the American people share with others all over the world who cherish freedom. Country by country, region by region, state by state, we have strengthened our public-safety efforts to make it much more difficult for terrorists.

Others have come to the forefront: from the Coast Guard to the Border Patrol, a wide range of agencies work day and night for our protection. Before the terrorist attacks of September 11, 2001, launched them into the spotlight, the courage of these guardians went largely unrecognized, although in truth, the sense of service was always honor enough for them. We can never repay the debt we owe them, but by increasing our understanding of the work they do, the *Rescue and Prevention: Defending Our Nation* books will enable us to better appreciate our brave defenders.

Steven L. Labov—CISM, MSO, CERT 3

Chief of Department, United States Search and Rescue Task Force

Left: The memorial to Oklahoma City's federal building records the minute before the morning bombing on April 19, 1995.

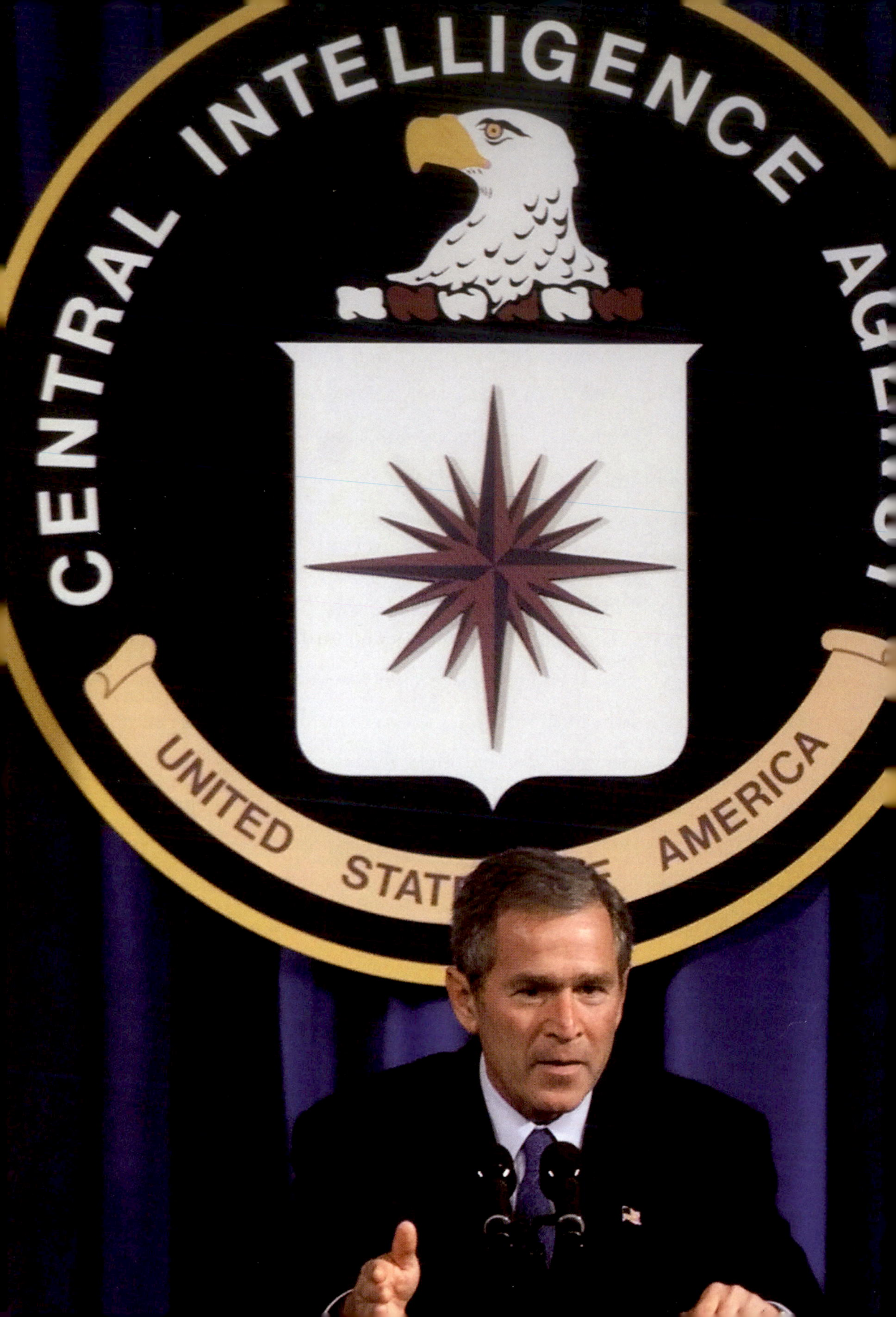
CENTRAL INTELLIGENCE AGENCY
UNITED STATES OF AMERICA

HISTORY OF THE CIA

Today's large and respected Central Intelligence Agency (CIA) grew out of smaller organizations formed to protect America's security in times of crisis. These groups seldom worked together, and no single government department analyzed their information. The CIA now has overall control of foreign intelligence, which includes spying.

The U.S. government has always collected secret information for national security purposes. Before World War II, those files reached the White House from the Department of State, the Federal Bureau of Investigation (FBI), and various special military units. These organizations, however, competed with one another instead of sharing their information. This departmental jealousy had to end when Adolf Hitler's Nazi regime waged war in Europe in the late 1930s. President Franklin D. Roosevelt created the Office of Coordinator of Information (COI) on July 11, 1941, and this agency later became the model for the CIA. Its first head, Major General William J. Donovan, is still called "the godfather of the CIA."

Donovan was known as "Wild Bill" because he had a dynamic character and loved action. This energy was certainly needed to organize the COI and ensure that it survived. When America

Left: President George W. Bush often praises the CIA's staff. "America relies upon your intelligence and your judgment," he told them. "I want to thank you for what you're doing."

entered World War II after the Japanese attacked Pearl Harbor on December 7, 1941, the Joint Chiefs of Staff wanted to break up the COI. Donovan, however, kept his organization together, operating independently, but reporting to the Joint Chiefs of Staff. On June 13, 1942, the COI became the Office of Strategic Services (OSS).

By late 1944, the OSS had nearly 13,000 employees, and some people joked that OSS stood for "Oh So Social" because it hired so many distinguished people. Its agents used devices of a type now associated with James Bond, such as cameras disguised as matchboxes, messages in hollowed-out silver dollars, and coat buttons holding a compass inside. The OSS also joined with Britain's Special Operations Executive (SOE) to fight **guerrilla campaigns** in Europe and Asia.

After the Allied victory, the U.S. government disbanded the OSS on October 1, 1945. However, two branches were saved—Secret Intelligence, which dealt with foreign intelligence; and X-2, whose task was **counterintelligence**. In January 1946, President Harry S. Truman combined them to form the Central Intelligence Group (CIG). The National Security Act of 1947 turned the CIG into the independent CIA, no longer under the Joint Chiefs of Staff.

The first CIA director was Rear Admiral Roscoe H. Hillenkoetter. He had an easier job than "Wild Bill" Donovan, because many of the employees had already been trained by the OSS. The agency now had to help contain **Communism** during the **Cold War** with the Soviet Union. The CIA looked for "the enemy within" the United States, and its overseas agents undertook dangerous **covert operations** to gather information, conducting a

Here William Donovan, "the godfather of the CIA," poses for a photograph. Today's agency is still influenced by Donovan's ideas about the intelligence service.

TERRORIST ATTACKS

In recent years, Americans have been subject to many terrorist attacks, even before the tragic events of September 11, 2001. The most infamous assaults are:

• October 23, 1983: A suicide bomber blows up Marine headquarters in Beirut, Lebanon, killing 241 Marines and Navy personnel.

• December 21, 1988: Libyans bomb Pan American Flight 103 over Lockerbie, Scotland, killing 270 people.

• April 19, 1995: Antigovernment activist Timothy McVeigh explodes a truck bomb outside the federal building in Oklahoma City, killing 168 people.

• August 7, 1998: U.S. embassies are bombed in Nairobi, Kenya, killing 291 people; and in Dar-es-Salaam, Tanzania, killing 10.

• October 12, 2000: A small ship carrying explosives rams the USS *Cole* off the coast of Yemen, killing 17 sailors.

• September 11, 2001: Islamic terrorists hijack four airliners, crashing two of them into the twin towers of the World Trade Center in New York City, killing more than 2,800 and destroying both skyscrapers. A third hits the Pentagon, causing 189 deaths; and a fourth crashes into the Pennsylvania countryside, killing all 45 on board, after passengers overpower the hijackers.

Left: Workers completed the cleanup of the World Trade Center debris in eight and a half months, finishing on May 30, 2002. They removed 1.8 million tons of rubble from Ground Zero.

President Harry S. Truman combined two intelligence agencies in 1946 to create the Central Intelligence Group, which became the CIA a year later.

"war of spies" with Soviet agents of the KGB. America's first real battle against Communist forces was the Korean War (1950–1953), when the CIA gathered military information using Korean and Chinese agents.

The 1960s began badly. The Russians shot down the CIA's U2 spy plane in 1960, and the next year, the agency was blamed for the Bay of Pigs failure, when it encouraged Cuban exiles in the United States to invade Communist Cuba. However, the CIA proved its worth in 1962, when a U2 flight discovered the Soviet missile buildup in Cuba, and President John F. Kennedy forced their removal. By the late 1960s, however, the agency had again lost the confidence of many Americans, who were protesting against the Vietnam War and questioning their government's role in the affairs of other nations.

Americans nevertheless turned again to the CIA in the 1980s to meet the rise of international terrorism. With the collapse of Communism in the 1990s, the agency could concentrate on finding hidden networks of terrorists. After the horrific attacks on America on September 11, 2001, the CIA quickly joined with the FBI and other organizations to lead the nation's counterterrorism efforts.

The U2 spy plane, developed by Lockheed, can fly as high as 75,000 feet (22,860 m) on reconnaisance missions. One discovered Soviet missiles in Cuba in 1962.

THE CIA'S ORGANIZATION

The CIA is an independent intelligence agency whose mission is to support the president, the National Security Council, and other officials involved in national security. Its headquarters are the George Bush Center for Intelligence in McLean, Virginia, on the Potomac River, seven miles (11 km) from Washington, D.C.

The head of the CIA is the Director of Central Intelligence (DCI). This person leads the nation's intelligence community and is the main advisor to the president for matters involving national security. George J. Tenet became the DCI on July 10, 1997, and it was he who oversaw the rapid expansion of the CIA after the terrorist attacks of September 11, 2001. He is assisted by a deputy director, who also serves as director when Tenet is on leave.

The CIA is organized into three teams, called directorates, which are in turn supported by various offices. The agency's three directorates are the Directorate of Operations (DO), the Directorate of Science and Technology (DS&T), and the Directorate of Intelligence (DI). The first two collect information that the Intelligence team then analyzes. All three receive special assistance from the CIA's five Mission Support Offices.

The best-known team is the Directorate of Operations, because

Left: George J. Tenet became CIA director in 1997. After September 11, 2001, he said the agency had the task of "unmasking the authors and sponsors of this evil."

its employees are the spies that protect national security. Each spy is officially known as an operations officer in the field, or just an operative. Humorously nicknamed "spooks," they are intelligence experts who are well educated and can speak at least one foreign language. They are sent undercover into other countries to recruit and work with foreign agents. Their secret assignments, which are often dangerous, involve collecting "human intelligence," or "HUMINT"—to use the CIA's term. These officers do invaluable work for their nation, but they know this will not be recognized outside the CIA, not even by their own families.

The CIA also uses spies that are not human. The United States has the greatest Signals Intelligence (SIGINT) in the world, made up of spy satellites and planes and other electronic devices. The Directorate of Science and Technology processes these photographs and information. These officers are usually scientists and engineers who are "tasked" (as they say) to create and use new technology

Left: Allen Dulles was the CIA director from 1953 to 1961. He resigned after the CIA supported the unsuccessful invasion of Cuba's Bay of Pigs.

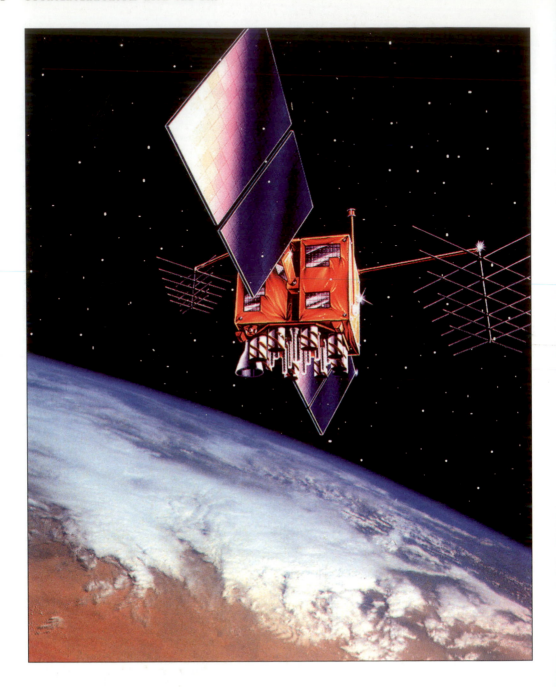

NAVSTAR global positioning satellites (GPS) are used by the U.S. armed forces. They guide aircraft, missiles, ships, and troops to targets that have often been located by the CIA's Magnum electronic intelligence satellites.

The CIA headquarters at McLean, Virginia, looks like a college campus. Besides offices, it has a company store, fitness center, food court, and other facilities.

systems, such as laser communications and video enhancements. But the DS&T staff also collects intelligence from other countries' television, radio, newspapers, and magazines, as well as their computer and telephone networks. The CIA calls these "open sources" because they are available to anyone, and the team's experts are trained to recognize threats to the nation in reported news events and political statements. They can also intercept threats by radio, phone, Web sites, and e-mail.

CIA officers divide the collected information into five different types to solve security questions and problems:

Nine Mile Point Nuclear Station in Scriba, New York, is one of the nation's nuclear facilities receiving additional security against terrorist attacks.

- Current intelligence: daily information and events
- Estimative intelligence: an analysis of possible dangers to come
- Warning intelligence: information that contains an urgent alert to danger
- Research intelligence: an in-depth study of a particular issue
- Scientific and technical intelligence: an analysis of foreign technologies, such as rocket programs

The Directorate of Intelligence brings together all this information, interpreting it and writing reports for the president and other people involved in national security. Each DI analyst has one or more areas of expertise and works on key foreign issues. Jobs include counterterrorism analysts and missile proliferation analysts.

THE SPY WITH A LIMP

The woman who retired from the CIA in 1966 could have been anyone's favorite grandmother. She was, in fact, one of history's most successful agents. Born in Baltimore, Virginia Hall studied languages and worked in the U.S. embassy in Warsaw, Poland.

Despite losing her left leg after a hunting accident, she joined the British Special Operations Executive during World War II and was sent to France to establish a spy network in Vichy. This she managed, also helping prisoners of war to escape. Pursued by the Nazis, she escaped by foot over the Pyrenees Mountains to Spain.

Virginia then joined "Wild Bill" Donovan's Office of Strategic Services as a radio operator and returned to France. Told that the Nazi's brutal secret police force, the Gestapo, was determined to find the "woman with the limp," she taught herself to walk without one. At night, she trained and led French resistance forces in guerrilla warfare and sabotage, coordinating air-drops for the D-Day invasion of France on June 6, 1944.

In 1945, Virginia became the only woman civilian to be awarded America's Distinguished Service Cross. After the war, she became one of the CIA's first female operations officers, serving her country for another two decades.

Each employee must tie together many puzzling strands of information, read between the lines, and meet strict deadlines for writing reliable and easily understood intelligence reports for policy makers, who are the nation's leaders.

COUNTERTERRORISM AT THE CIA

The American government has official definitions for terrorism and terrorists. The Code of Laws of the United States defines terrorism as "violence by groups or their secret agents against citizens who are not in the military."

Terrorist attacks are usually intended to influence opinions about governments and their politics. "International terrorism" is described as "terrorism involving the territory or the citizens of more than one country"—and in practice means that the person or group involved belongs to one nation and commits acts of terrorism in another nation. A "terrorist group" is any group that practices international terrorism. The job of the CIA and other U.S. counterterrorist organizations is to anticipate and defend against such attacks within America and overseas. The targets may be embassies, companies, U.S. citizens, or military personnel— about 250,000 members of the armed forces are stationed overseas at any one time.

President George W. Bush says that the CIA "serves as our ears and our eyes all around the world." It is certainly the nation's main agency for providing warnings of planned attacks directed from outside the United States.

Left: FBI agents looked for evidence after a hijacked airliner crashed into the Pentagon on September 11, 2001. The Defense Intelligence Agency (DIA) is located in the building.

THWARTING TERRORIST PLANS

The best way to discover terrorist plans is to make use of spies, who **infiltrate** their networks. To do this, CIA agents often use NOCS, "nonofficial-cover" officers who have no connection to the U.S. government. These NOCs have often committed crimes or even been terrorists themselves. It may seem irresponsible to use such people, but they are more easily accepted by terrorist rings and can help stop large disasters. Some CIA officers choose the more dangerous option of penetrating the networks themselves. They first learn the terrorists' language and live among them to understand their culture and organization. In both types of infiltration, the next vital steps are to disrupt and stop the attacks at the earliest possible stage. The CIA looks for weaknesses in terrorist groups and tries to hurt their structures, which might mean anything from destroying their communication system to cutting off their support from countries such as Iraq and Libya. To totally defeat the terrorists, the CIA might have to pursue them in other nations, like Afghanistan, Pakistan, and the Philippines.

The CIA runs the nation's counterterrorism program from the DCI Counterterrorist Center (CTC), located on the sixth floor of the agency's building in Virginia. The headquarters compound looks like a college campus, and is named the George Bush Center

Left: CIA Director William Casey established the agency's Counterterrorist Center (CTC) in 1986 to "preempt, disrupt, and defeat terrorists." At the age of 67, Casey was the CIA's oldest director. He earlier served in the Office of Strategic Services (OSS).

for Intelligence because the first President Bush headed the CIA for a year, from January 30, 1976 to January 20, 1977.

The DCI Counterterrorist Center is headed by the CIA director (DCI), who is also in charge of the entire intelligence community, consisting of 13 organizations. CTC employees work side-by-side with CIA people. The CTC was formed in 1986 by CIA Director William Casey after the U.S. government decided America was not aggressive enough in trying to stop and defeat terrorist activities. The CTC, which now has a staff of 1,000 employees, began with only three men in a single room with one television set.

The CTC is especially powerful because it draws upon not just the resources of the CIA, but also experts from other government agencies, including the FBI, the Department of Defense, and the National Security Agency. CTC staff includes intelligence officers and specialists, such as explosive experts and hostage negotiators. This combination has yielded many successes. Monitoring one terrorist group, Hizballah, the CTC was able to break up three planned attacks in the Middle East from 1999 to 2001. *Time* magazine noted on March 11, 2002, "The CTC is everything the rest of the intelligence community is not: coordinated, dynamic, and designed for the post-Cold War threat."

The CTC has a computer system called Desist, which stores facts

Right: The CIA and other U.S. government agencies have accused Saddam Hussein, the president of Iraq, of supporting international terrorism and developing weapons of mass destruction. President George W. Bush named Iraq a "rogue state."

The terrorist attack on the Pentagon destroyed 40,000 square feet (3,716 sq m) of building space. Rebuilding, the "Phoenix Project," began on November 19, 2001, with 600 workers. Their fast work was ahead of the scheduled completion date of September 11, 2002.

about known terrorists, including their photographs, fingerprints, and dental records. A File of International Terrorist Events (FITE) is also kept. This helps analysts predict future actions by terrorists based on the way they have behaved in the past. After Iraq invaded Kuwait in 1991, the CTC recorded about 120 attacks and threats in a few months. In the 1990s, about one-third of all terrorist attacks were against U.S. citizens and interests.

AN IMPERFECT BUSINESS

After the attacks of September 11, 2001, the Senate and others criticized the CIA and FBI for not providing a warning and not being able to prevent them. George Tenet, the CIA director, said his agency had already stopped three or four attacks during the summer before September 11, but added, "There's no perfection in this business." He said the agency knew that Osama bin Laden's Al Qaeda terrorist network might attack the United States, but was not aware of the intended targets. This is because secret attacks are often planned and known by only a handful of terrorists. And they may be people who are difficult to spot, like lone militants, **nonstate actors**—who operate without official national support—or "sleepers," who may behave normally for several years before suddenly launching an attack.

CIA officials announced in June 2002 that the agency was forming a new paramilitary unit to deal specifically with terrorists overseas. It will be under the command of the CIA's Counterterrorism Center and draw personnel from an existing paramilitary force within the agency's Special Activities Division.

The CIA's counterterrorism team also keeps track of the links that terrorists make with other enemies of the **Free World**. **Arms** dealers and criminal organizations, such as the Russian mafia, are eager to sell weapons to terrorists, including materials that might be used to develop nuclear bombs. Terrorists are known to have also made deals with drug traffickers to raise money. Afghanistan, a recent supporter of Osama bin Laden, is a major producer of opium and marijuana, and this helped fund his network.

Another problem comes from nations that support terrorists, such as Iraq, Sudan, and Libya. The U.S. government calls these "rogue states." A rogue is a wild and dangerous animal that wanders off from its herd, and these countries have gone their own way to endanger the world. In 2002, President George W. Bush used a new term for Iraq, Iran, and North Korea, calling them "an axis of evil" that is trying to develop WMD (weapons of mass destruction) to endanger democratic nations.

Finally, of special concern to the CTC are America's vast computer-based information systems. CIA Director George J. Tenet testified to Congress in 2001 that no nation in the world rivals the United States in its dominance of information systems and its reliance and dependence on them. **Cyber-attacks** by terrorists are likely, and their targets could be America's military, economic, or telecommunications systems. These are vital parts of the nation's **infrastructure**, and their destruction would halt practically all activity in America. Terrorists, for instance, could hack into Pentagon computers to steal secrets, or send viruses to crash the system, slowing or disrupting combat operations. The CIA has warned that the global expansion of information technology makes

Right: U.S. Secretary of Defense Donald Rumsfeld has coordinated America's military response to the September 11, 2001, attacks. "What we're doing," he said, "is trying to find the terrorists around the world who are trained to kill innocent men, women, and children."

WEAPONS OF MASS DESTRUCTION

In the past, terrorists have tended to use bombs, but the CIA is now increasingly concerned about the more dangerous threats posed by WMD, also known as CBRN—chemical, biological, radiological, and nuclear agents. The CIA knows that Osama bin Laden has trained members of his Al Qaeda terrorist organization to use chemical and biological poisons; and also that other groups, including Hamas, the Palestinian Islamic terrorist movement, are trying to develop their own chemical weapons.

The fear is that these methods can be used to poison the nation's food and water supply or even the air we breathe. After the attacks of September 11, 2001, the dangerous anthrax bacterium was mailed to several people, killing five and infecting 17 others who inhaled it. The government immediately implemented emergency plans to combat future attacks, which might use such deadly diseases as smallpox.

A planned chemical attack was recently thwarted. Its target was the U.S. embassy in Rome. In February 2002, Italian police arrested a terrorist cell of four Moroccan men during a predawn raid on their apartment. There they found the poison cyanide and a map of the city's water supply, with the U.S. embassy circled in red.

Right: Sheik Ahmad Yassin (front) is the spiritual head of Hamas, the Palestinian Islamic terrorist movement that he helped establish in 1987. Although paralyzed, he is known for his powerful and fiery speeches.

The CIA helped the French authorities capture the international terrorist "Carlos the Jackal," whose real name is Ilich Ramirez Sanchez. He was imprisoned for killing three people in 1975 and for kidnapping OPEC oil ministers in Vienna.

America more open to cyber-attacks, and the CTC is helping create ways to protect computer networks.

SHARING INFORMATION

As we have seen, it is essential that the CIA has a global reach. Its CTC works 24 hours a day to defeat terrorists, guided by the U.S. government's four-part policy: increase the counterterrorism programs of friendly nations; isolate nations that sponsor terrorism and put pressure on them to end their support; offer no deals to terrorists; and help bring them to justice.

To ensure success, the agency shares information with foreign intelligence services in friendly countries around the world. The CTC monitors the travel of terrorists—checking airplane tickets is one method—and then alerts the countries they plan to visit. From 1998 to 2002, the CIA worked with foreign governments to bring more than two dozen terrorists to justice. More than half of these were connected to Osama bin Laden's Al Qaeda organization.

The CIA, for instance, helped the French security service capture Carlos the Jackal, the most notorious terrorist prior to Osama bin Laden. He was a hit man for the Popular Front for the Liberation of Palestine and claimed to have killed 83 victims. In 1975, he took 11 oil ministers captive in Vienna. "I am the famous Carlos," he told them, adding, "To get anywhere, you have to walk over the corpses." In the 1980s, he bombed a high-speed train outside Paris and also bombed several buildings. Carlos never slept twice in the same place, but the CIA eventually located him. The agency cannot arrest terrorists in other countries if they have not committed crimes against the United States; so the CIA informed the French, who captured him in 1994.

CIA counterterrorist experts also work closely with the FBI to bring terrorists to justice. In 1987, the CTC helped the FBI track down the Lebanese terrorist who hijacked and blew up a Royal Jordanian airliner in Beirut. A year later, the two agencies joined together under the CIA's leadership to investigate the 1988 bombing of Pan American Flight 103 over Scotland, collecting evidence that led to the conviction of a Libyan terrorist in 2001 by a Scottish court. Then, in 1999, hard work by a CIA-FBI team stopped bombings planned by Osama bin Laden and others that might have killed thousands of Americans during the millennium celebrations. Instead, working with foreign governments, they disrupted terrorist groups in eight nations and made arrests in four: the United States, Canada, Pakistan, and Jordan. A year later, after the bombing of the USS *Cole*, the CIA and the FBI sent agents to Yemen. This operation was led by a top CIA official who had been a **liaison** in counterterrorism operations at the FBI headquarters.

In every case, the CIA agents explained the international situation to the FBI agents, who normally handle law enforcement cases within the United States. Following the Yemen investigation, Dale Watson, assistant director of the FBI's Counterterrorism Division, said, "The CIA guys helped us get the lay of the land. They steered us to the right people to talk to, told us who we needed to see, and explained what might offend people in the local culture." In 1996, the two organizations began exchanging senior officers from their counterterrorist offices to improve the conviction rate.

THE OKLAHOMA CITY BOMBER

We tend to think that terrorists attacking American targets are foreigners. Most attacks that take place in the United States are, however, committed by U.S. citizens. FBI records for the years between 1980 and 2000 show that three-quarters of the 335 suspected terrorist attacks were by Americans—some were members

FBI agents train as marksmen for their dangerous task of capturing terrorists and criminals. The FBI Academy on the U.S. Marine Base at Quantico, Virginia, has nine firing ranges and a rifle range.

of extremist groups; many were mentally unstable criminals.

Before September 11, 2001, the most destructive terrorist attack in the United States had cost the lives of 168 people, including 19 children. They died, and 850 more were injured, when a truck bomb destroyed the Alfred P. Murrah Federal Building in Oklahoma City on April 19, 1995.

Local police quickly caught the suspect, Timothy McVeigh. The investigation that followed, however, was headed by the FBI, the

Timothy McVeigh (wearing orange prison overalls) was arrested for the Oklahoma City bombing on April 21, 1995. Convicted, he was executed on June 11, 2001, at the federal penitentiary in Terre Haute, Indiana.

agency that handles terrorism within the United States. It formed an Okbomb Task Force, and its 56 field offices helped collect evidence. The investigation was one of the most intense in the agency's history, involving more than 28,000 interviews, over 238,000 photographs, 23,290 items of evidence, and millions of pages of records. The agency's experts testified at the trial, linking McVeigh to the evidence. An FBI chemist found traces of an explosive on the man's clothing, and another FBI expert found his fingerprints on a receipt for bomb materials. McVeigh was found guilty and executed. Terry Nichols, who assisted him, was sentenced to life.

The Oklahoma City bombing changed the way the FBI operates against terrorist groups. Before, it had to prove a particular federal crime had been, or was about to be, committed. After this case, the FBI can now act even if an extremist group was guilty only of discussing committing violent acts; such plans are discovered by operatives who have informants or who have themselves infiltrated terrorist organizations.

OSAMA BIN LADEN

"Dead or alive"—President George W. Bush has said that the United States wants Osama bin Laden one way or the other. This comment was made in response to the attacks of September 11, 2001. Prior to this, most Americans had never heard of bin Laden, the wealthy Arab extremist who is now the most wanted terrorist in the world.

The CIA and FBI, however, already knew a great deal about Osama bin Muhammad bin Awad bin Laden. By 1996, the CIA's CTC had named him as their leading target. Two years later, the CIA and U.S. Special Forces had a secret plan to capture bin Laden in his Afghanistan hideout, but this was never carried out because of concerns about the number of possible casualties. Within months, the U.S. embassies in Kenya and Tanzania had been bombed, and a federal grand jury charged bin Laden with murder. The FBI placed him on its "Ten Most Wanted Fugitives" list on June 7, 1999, and

Osama bin Laden, whose terrorist organization attacked the United States, disappeared when American-led forces bombed his Afghanistan hideouts in 2001 and 2002. It was uncertain if he had been killed or escaped.

the U.S. Department of State offered a $5 million reward for information leading to his capture—at that time the largest amount ever announced by the U.S. government for a fugitive.

Bin Laden was born in 1957 in Saudi Arabia, the son of a billionaire. When his father died in 1986, he inherited about $80 million. In 1979, he went to Afghanistan to fight against the Soviet invasion. The United States supported the anti-Soviet forces, but the CIA has strongly denied rumors that it ever worked with, or even met, bin Laden. After the Soviets were defeated, bin Laden returned to Saudi Arabia to work in his family's construction business. He was now a hardened Islamic fundamentalist who believed that Muslims should live by the religion's strict centuries-old doctrines.

When the United States and its allies fought the Persian Gulf War in 1991 against Iraq to liberate Kuwait, bin Laden became angry that U.S. forces were stationed in Saudi Arabia. He called it "an occupation of the land of the holy places." His arguments with the Saudi monarchy forced him to move that year to Sudan, but five years later, its government responded to U.S. pressure and expelled him. Bin Laden then returned to Afghanistan, and in 1996, issued a **fatwah**, calling on Muslims to kill U.S. troops, justifying this order by referring to Islamic law. Two years later, he included all American civilians as potential targets.

Protected by Afghanistan's Taliban government, bin Laden created a large terrorist organization that he called Al Qaeda, which means "the base." He built training camps for his followers—estimated to number about 3,000 fighters—and began the series of bombings against U.S. targets, which led to the September 11

In this photograph, F/A-18C Hornet ground-attack aircraft are launched from the U.S. Navy aircraft carrier USS *Carl Vinson* as part of the American campaign to rid Afghanistan of Al Qaeda terrorist training camps.

attacks that horrified the world. It also provoked a strong military response, which defeated the Taliban and scattered the Al Qaeda network. Bin Laden, after taping a few comments for television, disappeared. Dead or alive, he was gone. But as of this writing, America is still looking for him.

Left: Workers in the ruins of the World Trade Center towers had to proceed carefully among the dangerous debris. Many firefighters and policemen searched for their lost companions when the twin towers collapsed.

THE CIA'S WORK WITH OTHER COUNTERTERRORIST AGENCIES

The 13 organizations making up the intelligence community of the United States work together to warn political and military leaders of immediate and long-term threats. And they meet often to draw up plans to stop possible attacks.

The intelligence community shares its resources within the National Intelligence Council (NIC), which tries to predict future events. Pooling their knowledge, they also tap the knowledge of outside experts to decide what future events will affect national security. One of their recent publications, *Global Trends 2015*, estimates security threats up to that year.

The intelligence community includes the CIA and four government departments, as well as eight more answerable to the Department of Defense (DOD). The government bodies are the FBI, the Department of State, Department of the Treasury, and Department of Energy. Reporting to the DOD are the National Security Agency, Defense Intelligence Agency, National Reconnaissance Office, National Imagery and Mapping Agency, and the intelligence units of the Army, Navy, Air Force, and Marine Corps.

The FBI and CIA have worked closer together on terrorism since the September 11, 2001, outrage. FBI Director Robert Mueller announced in May 2002 that his agency would be reorganized to concentrate on terrorism.

THE FBI

The FBI is the CIA's most famous partner in counterterrorism. The FBI reports to the U.S. Department of Justice, and is the main law enforcement agency of the government, enforcing more than 200 federal laws. By contrast, the CIA has no real law enforcement function. It collects information about foreigners and their countries, but not about U.S. citizens, legal immigrants, resident aliens, or U.S. companies, regardless of where they are located.

The FBI began in 1908 as the Bureau of Investigation, a branch of the Department of Justice. In 1933, the Bureau changed its name to the Division of Investigation, and two years later, was renamed the Federal Bureau of Investigation. It started with 40 employees and today has nearly 30,000, of which about 11,400 are Special Agents. There are now 56 field offices and about 400 other offices, called "resident agencies."

The FBI became one of the world's best crime-fighting organizations under J. Edgar Hoover, who served as its director from 1924 until his death in 1972 at the age of 77. The agency is rightly known for its successful battles against organized crime. Its federal agents arrested the mob leader Al Capone in 1929, and shot and killed gangster John Dillinger in 1934. But the FBI has also defended the nation against spies and terrorists. In 1942, during World War II, German U-boats landed four agents on Long Island, New York, and four in Florida. Their mission was sabotage, aimed at damaging parts of the nation's infrastructure, but the Bureau arrested all eight. Two years later, another U-boat landed two Nazi spies in Maine, and again the FBI caught them both.

In 1998, former CIA Director John Deutch (right) and Secretary of Defense William Cohen unveiled a portrait of Les Aspin, a former Secretary of Defense. In 1997, Deutch called terrorism a disease that is spreading.

The FBI's "Ten Most Wanted Fugitives" list began in 1950. Osama bin Laden was the 456th name added to the list to make up the current "Ten Most Wanted." (It is worth noting that the FBI has apprehended or found 427 of the named fugitives.) On October 10, 2001, one month after the New York and Washington, D.C. attacks, the agency issued a "Most Wanted Terrorists" list with 22 names.

Traditionally, the CIA has investigated terrorism overseas, while the FBI has investigated cases within the United States. The increase

of global terrorist networks, however, has brought the agencies together. The FBI, therefore, has led or assisted investigations in many foreign countries and now has offices in more than 40 nations throughout the world.

When the U.S. embassy was bombed in Nairobi, Kenya, in 1998, the FBI immediately went there for the largest overseas operation in its history. It conducted more than 1,000 interviews during the investigation, code-named Kenbom (from "Kenya" and "bombing"). It also helped with the embassy bombing in Tanzania, and by 2001, this work led to 14 people being charged and four convicted and sentenced to life in federal prisons.

THE FBI'S COUNTERTERRORISM DIVISION

The Agency's Counterterrorism Division is located in the FBI building in Washington, D.C. Its Terrorist Research & Analytical Center uses a computer database called the Terrorist Information System (TIS), which has more than 200,000 terrorists and over 3,000 of their organizations on file. The Center can quickly retrieve information from this system to keep up with terrorists active in the United States and to forecast possible threats.

The Counterterrorism Division also heads two important organizations. The National Domestic Preparedness Office (NDPO) is

Left: J. Edgar Hoover was the FBI's first and longest-serving director, from 1924 to his death at the age of 77 in 1972. He developed it into a scientific crime-fighting agency with the world's largest fingerprint file.

The FBI maintains numerous heavily armed response units that can carry out antiterrorist operations at short notice.

America's center for information about terrorist weapons of mass destruction. It coordinates all federal efforts against these weapons and helps state and local groups plan emergency responses to possible attacks. The other agency is the National Infrastructure Protection Center (NIPC), which gathers information about terrorist threats to the nation's infrastructure. These threats are often attempts to disable the computer networks of the federal government and private companies. The NIPC investigates all such threats and acts to prevent them.

COMBINED EFFORTS

Besides the FBI, there are about 25 other governmental bodies working on counterterrorism. The State Department is the leading federal department dealing with international terrorism. It has an Office of Counterterrorism that develops new policies and works closely with foreign governments on intelligence. When serious international terrorist attacks happen, this office creates special task forces to coordinate the government's response. It also has the power to activate special military units for counterterrorism activities in other countries.

The department also keeps a computer file containing information about major terrorist incidents around the world, information on terrorist groups, and profiles of terrorists who might attack Americans. And its diplomatic security agents at every U.S. embassy work with foreign law-enforcement officials to prevent and respond to terrorist attacks on Americans.

The CIA also works with the Department of Energy, which has defense programs against chemical and biological attacks. It helped investigate the anthrax packages and letters sent to politicians and news media employees in September 2001. The department has nine laboratories around the country, which work with universities and businesses to develop devices that can sense dangerous materials. And they are also creating instruments to decontaminate a building or area that has been attacked. Indeed, the Pacific North-west National Laboratory has recently invented a machine that sprays a chemical fog that can render dangerous chemicals harmless.

Another important contact is the Department of the Treasury. The Treasury Enforcement Communications System (TECSII) is a computer database containing the descriptions and passport information of suspicious people entering the country. This system is linked to law enforcement databases kept in all 50 states.

The United States Customs Service is also a part of the Treasury.

The U.S. Coast Guard's security measures at ports were increased after September 11, 2001. Here, a Coast Guard HH-60J Jayhawk helicopter takes part in a combined operation with U.S. Marines in a combat raiding craft in Alaska.

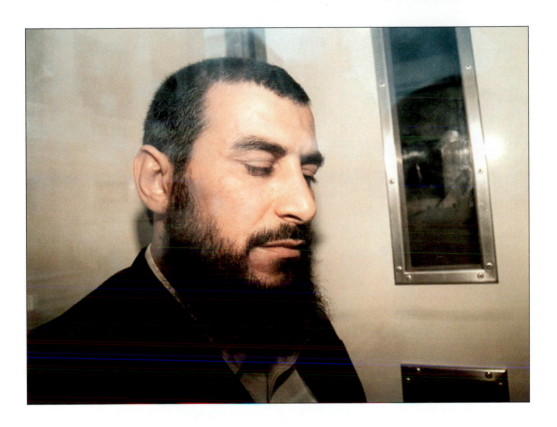

Ibrahim Eidarous was one of three London-based men indicted by the United States in 2001 for bombing the U.S. embassies in Kenya and Tanzania in 1998. The British government approved their extradition to America in 2001.

It has the important job of screening cargo to detect weapons, explosives, or bioterror agents, such as anthrax. U.S. ports handle over 17 million containers from ships every year, so the Customs Service is extremely busy.

The Treasury's Office of Foreign Assets Control has the power to freeze the U.S. bank accounts of known terrorists and even the bank accounts of nations that support them. It can also stop terrorists from moving money through American banks. This difficult job

Members of the Clinton administration participate in a Pentagon meeting of the National Security Council in 1998. Secretary of Defense William S. Cohen (center) briefs President Clinton and the Joint Chiefs of Staff on the situation in the Persian Gulf.

involves working with many foreign governments, but the Treasury has been joined by 150 other countries in blocking the flow of money that funds terrorism. Many frozen bank accounts belong to members of Osama bin Laden's Al Qaeda network.

Of special importance to Americans, since aircraft were used as weapons for the attacks of September 11, 2001, is the new Transportation Security Administration (TSA). It is now in charge of security operations at all 429 commercial airports in the United States, which includes screening passengers, baggage, and cargo. The

TSA, which is under the Department of Transportation, took over airport security duties on February 17, 2002. In its first few months, the new agency had to recruit 30,000 federal security personnel and 429 air security directors, as well as install bomb-detecting machines in the airports. It also took over security duties from the Federal Aviation Administration (FAA) and the airlines, which includes protecting secured airport areas and also the aircraft between flights.

Although the CIA issues terrorist alerts to the military, the Department of Defense has its own Defense Intelligence Agency (DIA), with headquarters in the Pentagon and more than 7,000 military and civilian employees worldwide. The intelligence units of the armed forces back up the DIA. The work of the DIA's employees is quite valuable to the counterterrorism activities of the CIA, FBI, and other organizations.

THE PRESIDENT, CONGRESS, AND THE CIA

The CIA coordinates the work of the intelligence community, but it must answer to both the president and Congress. The president's National Security Council (NSC), formed in 1947, reviews how well the CIA is doing and gives guidance on how its effectiveness can be improved. The president chairs the NSC, whose regular members are the vice president, the secretary of state, the secretary of the treasury, the secretary of defense, and the assistant to the president for national security affairs. The CIA director is the NSC intelligence advisor, while the chairman of the Joint Chiefs of Staff is the military advisor.

There is also the President's Foreign Intelligence Advisory Board

(PFIAB), made up of volunteer men and women who are not in government or the military. They look at the CIA from a business viewpoint—that is, they examine how well everybody works and how efficient the agency is. The members of this board receive no payment for their advice, which is valuable because of their experiences, achievements, and independence.

One other watchdog is the Intelligence Oversight Board. Its members help the president guarantee that the CIA's activities are legal and that it collects intelligence in a proper and responsible way, as outlined by the government.

Over in Congress, the CIA has to deal with several committees, and it has an Office of Congressional Affairs to help it do this. Two powerful committees can ask questions about counterterrorism: the Senate has a Senate Select Committee on Intelligence (SSCI) and the House of Representatives has a House Permanent Select Committee on Intelligence (HPSCI). Congress also has appropriations committees that can increase or cut back the CIA's funds. The various other committees that interact with the agency include those for foreign affairs, foreign relations, and armed services.

On February 14, 2002, the two Congressional committees announced a wide-ranging inquiry into why the CIA and other U.S. intelligence agencies did not know about the planned terrorist

Right: Workers in protective suits entered *The New York Times* building in Manhattan on October 12, 2001, to investigate a package containing powder. This was during the anthrax mail scare when the bacteria killed five people.

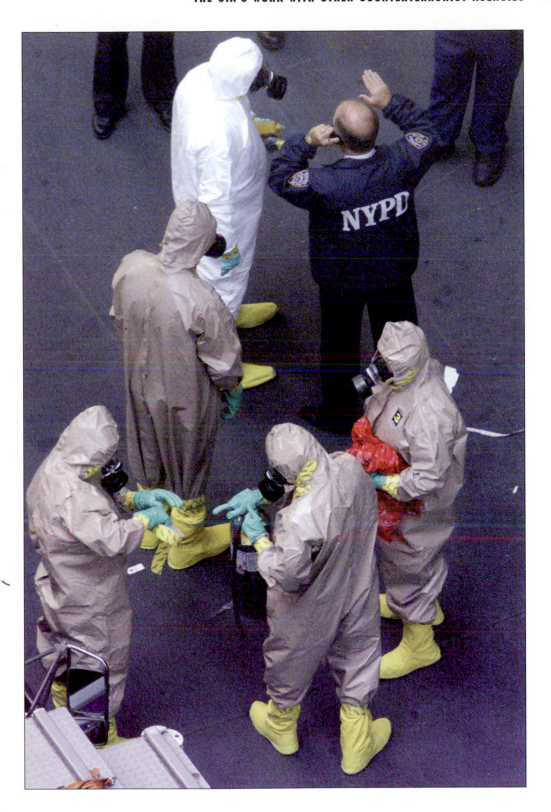

attacks of September 11, 2001, and were, therefore, unable to prevent them. A former CIA inspector general, L. Britt Snider, was put in charge of the investigation to see if changes are needed in the intelligence community to prevent further major attacks.

OTHER NATIONAL COUNTERTERRORIST AGENCIES

Most large nations have at least one security agency involved in intelligence gathering and counterterrorism. Britain has two, both located in London and coordinated by the prime minister's Cabinet Office. The Secret Intelligence Service (SIS), nicknamed "The Firm," has overseas spies who collect information on terrorist groups. It is usually still called by its former name, MI6, which stood for "Military Intelligence, Section Six." For more than 80 years (until 1994), the government would not officially admit that it even existed. The head of MI6 is always called "C" because a former director, Sir Mansfield Cumming, signed papers that way.

Working with MI6 is the Security Service, known as MI5, which is in charge of national security within Britain, collecting and analyzing intelligence about terrorist threats and countering them. This agency also cooperates closely with the country's other national security organizations, including the secret Government Communications Headquarters (GCHQ), and with law enforcement agencies, including the National Criminal Intelligence Service and local police forces. MI5 also has links with nearly 100 intelligence services worldwide.

The Canadian Security Intelligence Service (CSIS) took over intelligence gathering from the Royal Canadian Mounted Police

Harrison Ford tackles an armed and dangerous Irish Republican Army (IRA) terrorist in London, England, while playing CIA agent Jack Ryan in the movie *Patriot Games* (1992). Harrison Ford also played the same agent in another action movie, *Clear and Present Danger* (1994).

OLD COLD WAR ENEMY

The Komitet Gosudarstvennoi Bezopasnosti, or KGB (you can see why the initials were used), was an extremely powerful organization in the Soviet era. But it became defunct when Communism and the Soviet Union collapsed.

To operate its spy network worldwide, it had its own organization, the PGU—the Russian abbreviation for First Chief Directorate. Both organizations were replaced in 1991 after the collapse of Communism. The KGB became the Russian Federal Security Service—abbreviated to FSB in Russian. Vladimir Putin was head of the FSB from July 25, 1998, until August 9, 1999, before becoming Russia's president.

The PGU was renamed the Foreign Intelligence Service (SVR), which has a "Directorate T" in charge of counterterrorism. It established an Antiterrorist Center in 1995 to conduct these activities, and its main unit is called "Banner."

The next year saw 420 terrorist alerts. Many were bombs planted by Islamic terrorists and fighters from Chechnya, a region in the Caucasus region seeking independence. Russian troops, including the FSB's active unit named "Alpha," invaded Chechnya in 1994 and left in 1997 after claiming victory.

(the "Mounties") in 1984, and is now increasing its efforts to stop domestic terrorism. The Australian Secret Intelligence Service (ASIS) works in other countries to gather information.

Israel has an Institute for Intelligence and Special Tasks, named

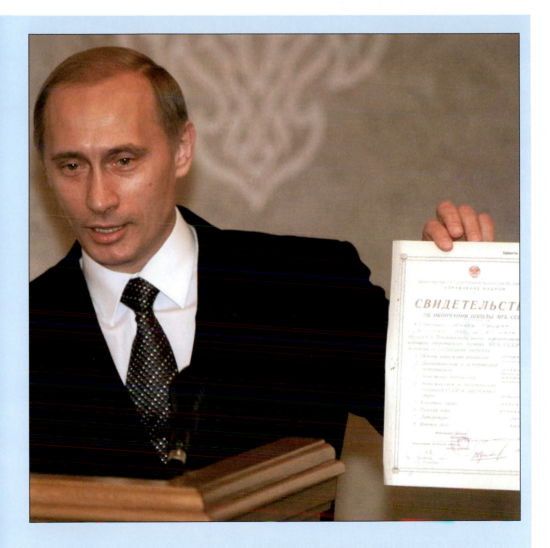

Russia's President Vladimir Putin gave full support to President George W. Bush's war on terrorism. Russia has also been the target of Muslim terrorists.

Mossad (meaning "institute" in Hebrew). Located in Tel Aviv, it was formed in 1951 and now has about 1,200 employees. Following the suicide bombings by Palestinian terrorist groups, like Hamas, the counterterrorism tactics of Mossad have included

Members of the president's National Security Council (NSC) staff analyze intelligence in the White House Situation Room. The CIA director is the intelligence advisor to the NSC, a body that also provides guidance to the CIA.

several **assassinations** of key members of those organizations, which has led to criticism.

Spain's intelligence service, which is run by the Ministry of Defense, is the Higher Center of Defense Intelligence (or CESID, as it is abbreviated in Spanish). It has developed counterterrorist methods to fight its own nation's terrorist organization, ETA, which was founded in 1959 and uses violence in an attempt to win a homeland for the Basque minority people. In the Basque language, ETA is short for "Basque homeland and liberty."

An Israeli postage stamp was issued in 1999 to honor Eli Cohen, who has been called "Israel's greatest spy." He worked for the Mossad intelligence agency.

CHANGES TO THE CIA AFTER SEPTEMBER 11, 2001

The terrible attacks that destroyed the World Trade Center towers and part of the Pentagon were viewed with disbelief. Nineteen Islamic terrorists had hijacked four airliners, using only cardboard cutters as weapons. How could the CIA and FBI, both renowned security agencies, have let such a large terrorist operation succeed?

Congress began an inquiry of public and private hearings. "We owe this to the 3,000 who died, their families, and the rest of America," said Senator Bob Graham, chairman of the Senate Intelligence Committee. At the same time, government officials said no piece of evidence had been uncovered that could have prevented the attacks.

Many rushed to defend the CIA and its counterterrorism program. The day after the attacks, CIA Director George Tenet reminded his employees of their past successes, saying, "Hundreds, if not thousands, of American lives have been saved by the brave men and women of our Counterterrorism Center, our Directorate of Operations, our analysts, our scientists, our support officers—all who work relentlessly every day against

Left: A police officer helps a detective escape the polluted air after the September 11, 2001, terrorist attack on New York's Twin Towers. By May 2002, officials had named 2,823 who died, including many police officers and firefighters.

New recruits for the Afghan National Army received uniforms and equipment on May 14, 2002. Intelligence work by the CIA aided the U.S. military effort that helped overthrow the Taliban regime.

this difficult target." President George W. Bush also visited the agency to say, "We've got the best intelligence we can possibly have thanks to the men and women of the CIA. America relies on your intelligence and your judgment."

Three months later, in December, the CIA prevented a series of attacks planned by Al Qaeda terrorists on the U.S. embassy, U.S. military forces, and other Western targets in Singapore. CIA agents found evidence of these plots on a videotape in Kabul, Afghanistan, and immediately alerted security officials in Singapore. One of the 13 suspects arrested said the attacks were to have been carried out the following week.

Testifying before Congress on February 6, 2002, Tenet said his agency had known since the summer of 2000 that bin Laden's network might attack targets on American soil, but it could not know all of the plots. "There is nothing we do that will guarantee 100 percent certainty. It will never happen." But the CIA had already made many changes to bring it closer to such perfection.

One swift move was to expand the Counterterrorist Center. It had doubled in size during the previous four years; in the four weeks after September 11, it doubled again. The CIA also began recruiting spies and other employees who had backgrounds in the languages and cultures of the Middle East, East Asia, and Central Eurasia (where Europe and Asia meet). These recruits were needed, not just to question both Taliban and Al Qaeda prisoners in Afghanistan and those held in Guantánamo Bay, Cuba, but also because terrorist materials found in Afghanistan were in such languages as Arabic, Urdu, Pashto, Chinese, and Russian.

The CIA and other agencies are cooperating more than ever on this new intelligence operation—the largest, most expensive, and most difficult one ever mounted by the United States. The government revised its national counterintelligence system in 2002, basing it on a new National Counterintelligence Executive (NCIX) formed to assess threats to the nation, plan the ways to counter them, and make sure information is shared by the different agencies. The president's budget for 2003 provides money for 60 existing agencies, including the CIA, FBI, and Coast Guard, to improve coordination through the Interagency Intelligence Committee on Terrorism. The budget also funds a new center to increase cooperation between the

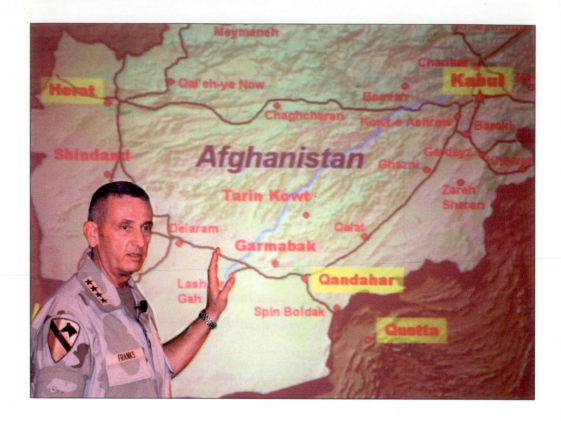

Army General Tommy R. Franks, commander-in-chief of the U.S. Central Command, briefed the press on November 27, 2001, on military operations in Afghanistan to locate and destroy Al Qaeda terrorist bases.

intelligence and law enforcement organizations. "This is the time for us to come together," CIA Director Tenet has said, "to bring all our talents to bear in a steely determination to do what we are called to do—protect our fellow citizens."

THE PRICE THE CIA PAYS

In the war to defeat the Taliban regime that supported Osama bin Laden, the CIA played an important role. Indeed, a CIA agent,

Johnny Michael Spann, was the first American to be killed on Afghanistan soil. He died on November 25, 2001, when Taliban prisoners he was interviewing attacked him at the desert fortress of Kala Jangi in the northern Afghan city of Mazar-e Sharif.

To honor him, the agency released his name—a highly unusual move. CIA Director George Tenet called him "an American hero, a man who showed passion for his country and his agency through his selfless courage." Spann had been in Afghanistan for just seven weeks when he was killed; many Afghans also died in the fighting.

Johnny Michael Spann, a CIA agent, was the first American killed in Afghanistan during U.S. military operations there. He was buried on December 10, 2001, at Arlington National Cemetery.

JOHNNY MICHAEL SPANN

Known to his friends as Mike, Johnny Spann was a friendly and kind young man. Popular for his dry sense of humor, great energy, and willingness to help others, he was also religious—his Church of Christ minister said, "His first priority in his life was to make sure he was right with God."

Spann grew up in the small town of Winfield, Alabama, where he played high school football. Graduating in 1987, he went on to earn a bachelor's degree from Auburn University and joined the Marines in 1992 for seven years, becoming a helicopter pilot. He was a captain when he left in 1999 for the CIA, which he had always dreamed of joining.

Spann was killed at the age of 32, leaving a wife and three children. He was buried in Arlington National Cemetery outside Washington, D.C. This cemetery holds the graves of more than 160,000 soldiers and others who have served their country, including President John F. Kennedy. The CIA director said Spann died where he wanted to be, "on the front lines serving his country," and he promised to continue "the mission Mike Spann held sacred....We owe that to Mike and to every man and woman who dreams of a future free of the menace of terrorism."

One of the prisoners Spann had interviewed that morning was John Walker Lindh, the American who had become a Muslim and gone to Afghanistan to fight with the Taliban. At the time of this writing, Lindh was being tried for terrorist offenses.

THE ANTHRAX ATTACKS

The September 11 attacks on America were quickly followed by another apparent terrorist tactic, the use of the deadly bacterium anthrax on civilians. Infection can occur if someone touches or eats anthrax spores, but the most dangerous form is "inhalation anthrax," by which the bacterium is simply breathed into the body. This causes a sore throat, fever, and muscle aches and, if diagnosed late, will sometimes lead to death. Until these anthrax attacks, only 18 cases had been reported in the United States since 1900, the last being in 1978. Now, an unknown terrorist was mailing anthrax to

Dr. Stephen Spear talked to reporters on November 21, 2001, in Derby, Connecticut, about his patient, Ottilie Lundgren, 94, who died later that day from anthrax.

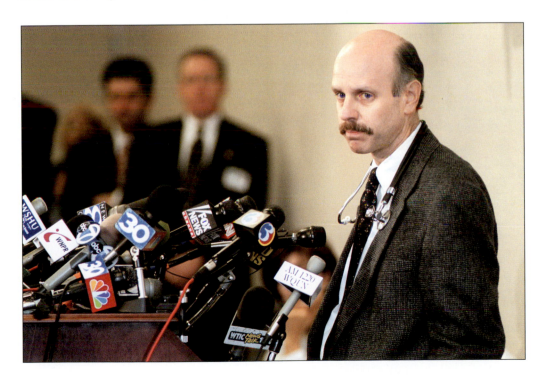

The U.S. post office in Seymour, Connecticut, delivered mail to Ottilie Lundgren, killed by anthrax. However, it was never determined how she came in contact with the bacterium.

politicians and news media people, killing four Americans in October 2001 and another in November 2001.

After the first victim was identified in Florida, about 50 federal, state, and local investigators came to the area, but no other evidence of anthrax was found. The next two victims were employees at the postal center that handled a package sent to Senator Tom Daschle. Two more employees at the center became ill, but survived, as did those members of the senator's staff that opened and handled the package. The fourth victim to die was a hospital worker, which meant that antibiotics had to be offered to the hospital's thousands of patients, employees, and visitors. In total, 18 people suffered from inhaling anthrax, including a worker at *NBC News* in New York and another senator.

Although anthrax cannot be spread from one person to another, the incidents caused widespread panic. Many people went to their doctors wanting protective antibiotics. The most commonly used one is Cipro, which should be taken only after infection, since it is itself dangerous otherwise. If the government wanted enough Cipro to protect against a mass anthrax attack, the cost has been estimated at $2.24 billion for a 60-day supply for 10 million people.

In the months following the attacks, FBI agents interviewed more than 500 people in laboratories. The powder sent in envelopes was analyzed, and seemed to indicate that it came from a U.S. laboratory. This suggested that the attacks were carried out by an American extremist who knew how to manufacture anthrax. As of this writing, the agency is continuing its investigations with the help of the U.S. Centers for Disease Control and Prevention.

VICTIMS OF ANTHRAX

In the fall of 2001, the anthrax attacks that spread fear across the United States cost the lives of five people.

Bob Stevens, 63, was the first person to die, on October 5. He was a photo editor in Lantana, Florida, for a supermarket newspaper that had strongly criticized Osama bin Laden. It was also noted that one of the terrorists aboard one of the planes that crashed into the World Trade Center had trained at an airport a few blocks away from where Stevens worked.

Two weeks later, two postal workers in Washington, D.C. died of inhalation anthrax. Thomas Morris, Jr., 55, and Joseph Curseen, Jr., 47, worked at a letter-processing center that had handled a letter containing anthrax powder sent to U.S. Senate Majority Leader, Tom Daschle.

The fourth person to die, on October 31, was Kathy Nguyen, 61, who worked in a supply room of the Manhattan Eye, Ear, and Throat Hospital in New York City.

The fifth victim was Ottilie Lundgren, 94, who died on November 21 in Oxford, Connecticut. She had no contacts with news or government offices or with postal facilities, and her exposure to the anthrax bacterium remains puzzling.

Right: The FBI released the note found with anthrax mailed to Tom Brokaw, the NBC anchor, and to the editor of the *New York Post*. The agency's hope that the handwriting would be recognized was not fulfilled.

09-11-01

THIS IS NEXT

TAKE PENACILIN NOW

DEATH TO AMERICA
DEATH TO ISRAEL

ALLAH IS GREAT

NEW U.S. COUNTERTERRORISM MEASURES

Just as the CIA has increased in scope and power since the attacks on America, other counterterrorism agencies have also received more support. New ones have also been established.

Congress created the Transportation Security Administration (TSA), as mentioned, to take over airport security throughout the United States; although the process was gradual, the transition was completed by the end of 2002. Explosive-detection equipment was installed by the end of 2002 to check all bags. The first year, funding for the TSA was $4.8 billion, which included $2.2 billion from passenger and air carrier fees.

Another new organization is the Office of Homeland Security, created on October 8, 2001. Its job is to strengthen the protections needed against terrorist threats or attacks in the United States. To do this, the new team will coordinate the counterterrorism efforts of the U.S. government, states, and local organizations. Tom Ridge, the former governor of Pennsylvania, has been appointed as its first head. He reports directly to the president and has the authority to manage

Left: Members of the Louisiana Air National Guard patrol outside the Superdome in New Orleans, February 2002. Security has been increased following the terrorist attacks of September 11, 2001.

THE HOMELAND SECURITY BUDGET FOR 2003

On February 4, 2002, President George W. Bush announced his proposed U.S. federal budget for 2003. Totaling $2.13 trillion, it includes $38 billion for defense and homeland security, an $18 billion increase over previous years. Issued by the Office of Management and Budget, it "reflects not just our absolute commitment to achieving a much more secure homeland, but also our determination to do so in a manner that preserves liberty and strengthens our economy." Details of the budget include:

● $3.5 billion to ensure that state and local "first responders" (firefighters, police, and rescue workers) are prepared for terrorism.

● $5.9 billion to enhance defenses against biological attacks.

● $380 million to establish a reliable system to track the entry and exit of immigrants.

● $722 million for improvement to information sharing within the federal government and between it and other organizations.

● $4.8 billion for the new Transportation Security Administration.

   The president added that guaranteeing homeland security is "a challenge of monumental scale…. It will not be cheap, easy, or quick…. Our work has already begun, and it will continue…[and] ultimately we will succeed in weaving a proper and permanent level of security into the fabric of America."

counterterrorism activities through all levels of government. The office's Homeland Security Council advises the president on U.S. security, and its 11 members include the heads of the CIA and FBI.

Bryan Fenley, a U.S. Border Patrol agent, uses an infrared camera at the top of a mesa to search for illegal aliens trying to enter from Mexico through Sunland Park, New Mexico.

On March 12, 2002, the homeland security director announced a new color-coded homeland security advisory system for federal agencies and state and local governments. Its five levels for terrorist attacks are:

- Green (low): for low risks
- Blue (guarded): for general risks
- Yellow (elevated): for significant risks
- Orange (high): for high risks
- Red (severe): for severe risks

    Ridge reported at that time that the United States was at the yellow level and would remain there for "the foreseeable future." He added that terrorism is now a permanent and ever-present threat.

The Pentagon was also given a larger homeland mission. U.S. military forces now help with air patrols to protect cities from new attacks. Military aircraft at bases in the United States were put on a strip alert of 15 minutes, meaning they could take off within 15 minutes to intercept a terrorist-controlled plane. The Pentagon also called up 35,000 members of the National Reserve to help the recovery efforts in New York and Washington, D.C. and for

In October 2001, Pennsylvania governor Tom Ridge was named the first head of the new Office of Homeland Security. It coordinates the federal, state, and local efforts to defend against terrorism.

Jeff Underwood of the U.S. Coast Guard patroled Boston Harbor on October 11, 2001. The service sent armed patrol boats to major U.S. ports after the September 11 attacks.

homeland defense. About 8,000 were stationed at baggage-screening points in 420 airports, and some 700 were assigned to join the Border Patrol along the United States' 4,000-mile border with Canada. Troops were also assigned to temporarily help other agencies, such as the Customs Service. The military also is setting up a new homeland command, named NORCOM, to overlook the North American Aerospace Defense Command (NORAD)—which tracks incoming aircraft and missiles—and to respond to real attacks by chemical, biological, or nuclear weapons.

U.S. Customs will be increased by 800 more agents. Some, for the first time, have been stationed outside the country, going to three Canadian ports—Vancouver, Montreal, and Halifax—to help screen cargo containers bound for the United States. Canadian customs inspectors also assist inspectors in Newark, New Jersey, and Seattle, Washington, for cargo destined for Canada. Plans are for U.S. Customs teams to screen cargo at the 10 busiest ports in the world. The Coast Guard's role in port security was also increased.

Since several of the September 11 terrorists had student visas, the U.S. Immigration and Naturalization Service (INS) activated a Student and Exchange Visitor Information System (SEVIS). This creates a database on students, who can then easily be tracked as they move around the United States. The information is also given to U.S. embassies. Another new INS program screens in advance all travelers entering from Canada; a device in their vehicle can be read at the border crossing to speed up processing. On the Mexican border, a laser visa system is planned that lets prescreened travelers swipe their cards in a machine. A larger tracking system is also planned for 2005 to trace all visitors from other nations that enter or leave U.S. air, sea, or land ports.

Overall, U.S. agencies made impressive moves during the first 100 days after September 11. A total of 93 antiterrorist task forces were created—one in each U.S. attorney's district—to bring

Security has been tightened in Washington, D.C., and in other major cities around the United States. This bomb search by a sniffer dog was conducted on February 22, 2002, at an underground parking lot near the White House.

Turkish special policemen guard a Hizballah guerrilla, Mahmut Demir (center, wearing a balaclava), in the city of Adana. He was being questioned by Chief Prosecutor Nuh Mete Yuksel.

together the communications and activities of federal, state, and local law enforcement.

TERRORIST ORGANIZATIONS

The U.S. Department of State has named 39 groups as terrorist organizations. The FBI established the new "Most Wanted Terrorist" list and a national task force to centralize information. This has led to hundreds of thousands of leads, more than 500

INTERNATIONAL TERRORIST ORGANIZATIONS

The Office of Counterterrorism releases a document called "Background Information on Foreign Terrorist Organizations." In 2002, there were 39 groups listed, including Osama bin Laden's Al Qaeda. Others mentioned are:

Abu Nidal Organization (ANO)

Also known as Black September, this group has carried out attacks in more than 20 countries, killing or injuring almost 900 people. Targets have included the United States, the United Kingdom, France, Israel, and moderate Arab countries. Its leader, Sabri al-Banna, may have relocated to Iraq in 1998.

Hizballah (Party of God)

A radical Shiite group formed in Lebanon, which is strongly anti-West and anti-Israel. Often directed by Iran, it has been involved in numerous attacks, including the suicide truck bombing of the U.S. embassy and Marine barracks in Beirut in October 1983.

Palestine Islamic Jihad-Shaqaqi Faction (PIJ): Originating among militant Palestinians during the 1970s, this is a loose affiliation of factions committed to the creation of an Islamic Palestinian state and the destruction of Israel through holy war.

Revolutionary People's Liberation Party

Formed in 1978 in Turkey, this group is strongly opposed to the United States. Terrorists assassinated two U.S. military contractors and wounded a U.S. Air Force officer to protest American involvement in the Persian Gulf War.

searches, and thousands of interviews; criminal charges have been served against 1,016 suspected terrorists. The government has offered a reward of up to $35 million for information leading directly to the capture or conviction of Osama bin Laden, and has also created a Foreign Terrorist Tracking Task Force to keep terrorists from entering the country and to find and remove members of terrorist networks. As well, the government moved quickly to protect Muslim citizens from hate crimes, investigating about 300 incidents and bringing federal charges in six cases.

On September 11, immediately after the attacks, President Bush moved to protect the federal government from a large-scale terrorism attack on the nation's capital, perhaps from "dirty nukes," portable devices that would spread radiation over a wide area. He also sent a "shadow government" of about 100 civilian workers to live, without their families, in secret underground locations outside Washington, D.C.

To provide continuity of government (COG), these officials from various departments and agencies could keep the federal government working to overcome communications, transportation, and other facilities damaged by such attack. This planning is handled by the new Office of Homeland Security.

Despite this defensive mood, the president, government, and nation remain confident of withstanding international terrorism and finally defeating it. Attorney General John Ashcroft said, "Our number one priority is the prevention of terrorist attacks." And President Bush reminded Americans that "the best way to fight terrorism is to not let terrorism intimidate America."

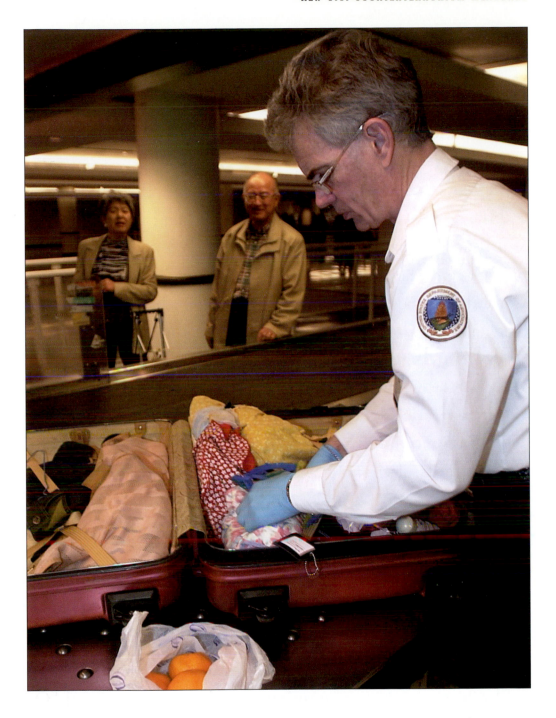

More luggage is now undergoing special checks by hand at the nation's airports. This examination was in December 2001 at Chicago's O'Hare International Airport.

GLOSSARY

Arms: a means (as a weapon) of offense or defense

Assassination: to murder by sudden or secret attack usually for impersonal reasons

Cold War: a period of sustained hostility between the United States and the Soviet Union; the situation lasted from the end of World War II until the late 1980s without either side resorting to outright military conflict

Communism: a system of government in which a single authoritarian party controls state-owned means of production

Counterintelligence: activities designed to collect information about enemy espionage and then to thwart it

Covert operations: secret plans and activities carried out by spies and their agencies

Cyber-attacks: electronic attacks on computers, often sent as e-mail viruses

Fatwah: a legal opinion or decree handed down by an Islamic religious leader

Free World: a name given to democratic countries collectively, traditionally used for Western nations

Guerrilla campaigns: hit-and-run fighting techniques used by small units that are not a part of the regular armed forces

Infiltrate: to penetrate an organization, like a terrorist network

Infrastructure: the crucial networks of a nation, such as transportation and communication, and also including government organizations, factories, and schools

Liaison: a person who establishes and maintains mutual understanding and cooperation between two groups

Militant: having a combative or aggressive attitude

Nonstate actor: a terrorist who does not have official government support

CHRONOLOGY

1941: July 11, President Franklin D. Roosevelt establishes the office of Coordinator of Information (COI), the model for the CIA.

1942: June 13, the COI becomes the Office of Strategic Services (OSS).

1945: October 1, the OSS is disbanded.

1946: January 22, President Harry S. Truman's directive establishes the Central Intelligence Group (CIG).

1947: July 26, the National Security Act of 1947 comes into effect, creating the independent CIA to replace the CIG; Rear Admiral Roscoe H. Hillenkoetter is the first director.

1949: The Central Intelligence Act of 1949 gives Congress authority to regulate the CIA.

1953: February 26, Allen Dulles becomes CIA director and serves until November 29, 1961.

1960: May 5, the Soviet Union downs a CIA U2 spy plane; the pilot, Gary Powers, survives and is exchanged for a Soviet spy in 1962.

1961: CIA-supported Cuban refugees invade Cuba at the Bay of Pigs and are defeated.

1962: October 14, a CIA U2 plane discovers Soviet missile sites in Cuba.

1976: January 30, former president George Bush becomes CIA director and serves until January 20, 1977.

1986: The CIA's Counterterrorist Center (CTC) is established by CIA director William Casey.

1988: December 21, Libyan terrorists bomb Pan American Flight 103 over Lockerbie, Scotland, killing 270; the CIA is placed in charge of the investigation.

1997: July 10, George J. Tenet is named CIA director.

1998: August 7, Islamic extremists bomb the U.S. embassies in Kenya and Tanzania; the CIA and FBI work together to track the terrorists.

2000: October 12, the USS *Cole* is bombed off Yemen, killing 17; the CIA leads the investigation.

2001: September 11, Islamic terrorists hijack four airliners; they fly two into the twin towers of the World Trade Center, destroying them, and one into a section of the Pentagon, causing a total of more than 3,000 deaths; the FBI and CIA link the attacks to Osama bin Laden and his Al Qaeda terrorist network.

2002: Director George J. Tenet attends talks with Palestinian Cabinet ministers in an attempt to begin the peace process in the West Bank of Israel.

FURTHER INFORMATION

USEFUL WEB SITES

The CIA: www.cia.gov; www.cia.gov/cia/ciakids/index.html

The FBI: www.fbi.gov

The National Intelligence Council: www.cia.gov/nic/index.htm

The National Counterintelligence Executive: www.ncix.gov

The Department of Defense: www.defenselink.mil/pubs/dod101

The Defense Intelligence Agency: www.dia.mil

For details of how "America Responds to Terrorism": www.white-house.gov/response

FURTHER READING

Baer, Robert. *See No Evil: The True Story of a Ground Soldier in the CIA's War on Terrorism*. New York: Crown Publishing, 2002.

Hamilton, John. *Operation Noble Eagle: The War on Terrorism*. Minneapolis: Abdo & Daughters, 2002.

January, Brendan. *The CIA*. Danbury, Connecticut: Franklin Watts, 2002.

Landau, Elaine. *Osama bin Laden: A War Against the West*. New York: Twenty First Century Books, 2002.

Louis, Nancy. *Osama bin Laden*. Minneapolis: Abdo & Daughters, 2002.

Melton, H. Keith. *The Ultimate Spy Book*. New York: DK Publishing, 1996.

Platt, Richard. *Eyewitness: Spy*. New York: DK Publishing, 2000.

Prados, John. *America Confronts Terrorism: Understanding the Danger and How to Think About It*. Chicago: Ivan R. Dee, 2002.

Smith, Dennis. *Report from Ground Zero: The Story of the Rescue Efforts at the World Trade Center*. New York: Viking Press, 2002.

ABOUT THE AUTHOR

Dr. John D. Wright is an American writer and editor living in England. He has been a reporter for *Time* and *People* magazines in their London bureaus, covering such subjects as politics, crime, and social welfare. He has also been a journalist for the U.S. Navy and for newspapers in Alabama and Tennessee. He holds a Ph.D. degree in Communications from the University of Texas, taught journalism at three southern universities, and was chairman of the Department of Mass Communications at Emory & Henry College in Virginia. In 2001, he published a dictionary, *The Language of the Civil War*, and an encyclopedia of space exploration is scheduled for publication in Great Britain. He has contributed to many reference books, including the Oxford University Press *New Dictionary of National Biography* (under production), Reader's Digest *Facts at Your Fingertips* (2001), and the *Oxford Guide to British and American Culture* (1999).

INDEX

Numbers in italics refer to illustrations